Modern Akan

A concise introduction to the Akuapem, Fanti and
Twi language

Modern Akan

A concise introduction to the Akuapem, Fanti and Twi language

kasahorow Editors

Modern Akan: a concise introduction to the Akuapem, Fanti and Twi language

by kasahorow Editors

Esi Cleland

Kofi Oteng Gyang

Nana Kodwo (Jojoo) Imbeah

Paa Kwesi Imbeah

Series: kasahorow Language Guides

ISBN 978 9988 0376 73
3rd Printing
©kasahorow.org. Nyia ɔ nnyim no sua a, ɔ hu.

ii

Contents

vi

List of Tables

Preface

All mistakes are ours.

Acknowledgments

Our sincere thanks to the following reviewers who helped to straighten out the explanations to make this a better book:

> Andrij Rovenchak

> Charles Riley

> Christiana Dankwa

License

You may freely photocopy and redistribute this book for private or commercial use. No restrictions. Yes you do not need our permission. Do good.

The ISBN for this book was kindly supplied by the Ghana Library Board, Accra.

Errata

The website for this book is
  `http://kasahorow.org/book/concise-akan`.
Please submit your feedback there or send us an email at
  `help+concise-akan@kasahorow.org`.

Typesetting

This book was was typeset with XeTeX. The font is Gentium Basic.

Chapter 1

Modern Akan

This short guide is designed to get you up to speed quickly with the modern Akan language. We hope that after getting through it you will be able to read, write and speak basic Akan sentences to express the following range of concepts:

1. I love you
2. Kwame and Kwesi are boys
3. John came here before I did
4. Who is that?
5. Adwoa will come home tomorrow
6. I came, I saw, I conquered
7. They do not like that
8. How did they eat five pizzas in two hours?
9. The family has entered their new house

10. Stop eating and hurry up!

For teachers of Akan, this guide should provide you a basic outline for getting your new language learners to master the basic structure of the Akan language. "Modern Akan" is the spelling system used in this book. Regional variations are purposely omitted from this guide except in the Speaking Akan chapter (4).

1.1 Some explanations

In the text, any text marked with * indicates ungrammatical usage. Bolded text can be looked up in the index. The guide attempts to use plain English the first time a concept is explained; in this case the technical term is included in square brackets.

Pronunciations are surrounded by /.../ signs.

Written form   a
Spoken form   /a/

English translations are placed in italics in [ ] near their Akan renditions.

1.1.1   Cover image

Nyia ɔnnyim no sua a, ɔhu [*The ignorant can learn*] is the literal meaning of the image in the kasahorow logo on the back page of this guide. The image represents an aphorism belonging to the larger set of

Adinkra symbols shown on the front page. The aphorism is better be translated into English as [*learning cures ignorance*] because it is normally used to inspire. It represents the urge to seek knowledge, to become less provincial and more cosmopolitan in taste. We hope that this guide will help open up the culture of the Akan peoples all over the world to you.

Chapter 2

Reading Akan

The easiest way to learn the rules [**grammar**] of a language is to read text written in that language. This section will help you analyse Akan texts to extract meaning from them.

In the past Akan text was written exactly the way it was spoken. This means that a lot of old material may be hard to read if you are not familiar with the pronunciation style of the writer. However, modern Akan is written in a consistent way regardless of the writer's pronunciation. Chapter 3 has more details of how modern Akan is written. This chapter teaches you how to read modern Akan text. A good example of modern Akan text can be found in the Akan versions of popular websites such as Google [1] and software such as Firefox [2].

2.1 Recognising letters

Akan is written with 26 letters [**alphabet**] (Table 2.1). The letters enclosed in parentheses are mainly used in words imported from other languages (usually scientific notation).

Aa	Bb	(Cc)	Dd	Ee	Ɛɛ
Ff	Gg	Hh	Ii	(Jj)	Kk
(Ll)	Mm	Nn	Oo	Ɔɔ	Pp
Rr	Ss	Tt	Uu	(Vv)	Ww
Yy	Zz				

Table 2.1: Akan alphabet

2.2 Recognising words

The main types of words [**parts of speech**] used in Akan are those that represent persons, places, things or ideas [**nouns**], and actions [**verbs**].

2.2.1 Nouns

The nouns in any language are unlimited. Everything that has a name is a noun. Nouns can be represented by a single word or a group of words. Languages grow by making up new nouns to represent new things.

There are two main types of Akan nouns:

- **regular nouns**, and

- **person nouns**.

When there is just one item of the noun [**singular**] or the noun cannot be counted, you do not need to modify the spelling in any way. When there is more than one [**plural**] of the noun, the spelling is modified to indicate this.

Regular nouns and person nouns form their plurals differently.

Regular nouns

Regular nouns form their plurals by adding **n** to the beginning of the singular noun. If the singular noun starts with *m, b, p* or *f*, the plural is formed by adding **m** to the beginning of the singular noun.

	Singular	Plural	Singular	Plural
Akan	kua	**n**kua	busua	**m**busua
English	farm	farms	family	famil**ies**

Person nouns

Person nouns end [**suffix**] in **nyi** (Akuapem & Twi /ni/; Fanti /nyi/) when referring to the singular. When

referring to the plural, **nyi** is replaced by the usual
n or **m** at the beginning [**prefix**] and **fo** at the end.

	Singular	Plural	Singular	Plural
Akan	kua**nyi**	**n**kua**fo**	busua**nyi**	**m**busua**fo**
Lit. Eng.	farm-	farm-	family-	family-
	person	**persons**	**person**	**persons**
English	farmer	farmers	relative	relatives

2.2.2 Determiners

Definite articles come after the noun. Indefinite articles are optional: if present, they are prefixed to
the noun.

- **definite articles**
  banyin <u>**no**</u> [*the* boy] banyin <u>**bi**</u> [*some* boy]

- **indefinite articles**
  banyin [<u>*a*</u> boy, or, boy] **panyin** [<u>*an*</u> adult, or, *adult*]
  <u>**ɔ**</u>panyin [<u>*an*</u> adult] <u>**ɔ**</u>kraman [<u>*a*</u> dog]

2.2.3 Pronouns

Happily, pronouns can stand in for any noun. The
common pronouns are explained below.

Subject pronouns usually replace a noun at the
beginning of a sentence. A subject pronoun comes
before a verb. The verb replaces the tilde '∼' after the pronoun 2.2, for example, **Me** *dɔ* wo [*I love*

Akan	me ~	e ~, wo ~	ɔ ~
English	I	you	she, he, it
Akan	yɛ ~	hom ~, mo ~	wɔ ~
English	we	you (plural)	they

Table 2.2: Subject pronouns

you]. In older texts, the pronoun is usually written together with the verb as **Medɔ wo**.

Akan	me	wo	no
English	me	you	her, him, it
Akan	yɛn, hɛn	hom, mo	wɔn, hɔn
English	us	you (plural)	them

Table 2.3: Object pronouns.

Object pronouns usually replace a noun anywhere else apart from in the beginning of a sentence. Object pronouns, listed in Table 2.3, are written alone, for example, Gye ma **me** [*Get it for **me***].

Possesive pronouns attribute ownership to someone or something. Possessive pronouns, listed in table 2.4, are written alone, for example, Gye **me** aduane no [*Get **my** food*].

Interrogative pronouns, listed in Table 2.5, are used to ask questions, for example, **Woana** nye no? [***Who** is he/she?*].

Akan	me	wo	ne
English	my	your	her, his, its
Akan	yɛn, hɛn	hom, mo	wɔn, hɔn
English	our	your (plural)	their

Table 2.4: Possessive pronouns.

Akan	English
woana	who
dɛn	what
adɛn	why
hemfa	where
sɛn	how
bɛn	which

Table 2.5: Interrogative pronouns.

2.2.4 Verbs

There are two important things to look for in Akan verbs:

- an indication of the period of time in which the action took place [**tense**],

- an indication of whether the opposite action is being described [**negation**].

Action taking place now or habitually

For actions taking place at the time of speaking [**simple present tense**], or that take place on a regular basis [**habitual tense**], the verb has no special indicator of time. This is the form of the verb found in dictionary entries.

Akan	Me **ba**	Kofi **ba**
English	I **come**	Kofi **comes**

Table 2.6: Simple present, habitual tense.

Action took place in the past

This is the **simple past tense**. If the verb is not the last word in the sentence, the simple past is indicated in speech by stressing the last letter of the verb. However, if the verb is the last word in the sentence, the simple past is indicated by stressing the last vowel in the verb. This difference is not distinguished in Modern Akan writing. In writing, the simple past tense is simply indicated by adding a **ee** to the simple present tense form of the verb.

Akan	Me **baee** ndeda	Esi **baee** ndeda
Speech	Me /**baa**/ ndeda	Esi /**baa**/ ndeda
English	I **came** yesterday	Esi **came** yesterday
Akan	Me **baee**	Esi **baee**
Speech	Me /**bae**/	Esi /**bae**/
English	I **came**	Esi **came**

Table 2.7: Simple past tense.

Action has taken place

This is the **present perfect tense**. The present perfect tense is indicated by inserting **a** [*has, have*] in front of the verb.

Akan	Me **a**ba	Ama **a**ba
English	I **have** come	Ama **has** come

Table 2.8: Present perfect tense.

Action is taking place

This is the **present continuous tense**. It is indicated by inserting **re** [*is in the process of*] in front of the verb.

Akan	Me **re**ba	Ama **re**ba
English	I **am** coming	Ama **is** coming

Table 2.9: Present continuous tense.

Action will take place in the future

This is the **simple future tense**. The future tense is indicated by inserting **bɛ** [*will*] in front of the verb.

Akan	Me **bɛ**ba	Ama **bɛ**ba
English	I **will** come	Ama **will** come

Table 2.10: Future tense.

Action happens in the near future

This tense is the near future tense. It is indicated by **kɔ** [*go*] in front of the verb.

Akan	Me **kɔ**da	Ama **kɔ**da	
English	I **go to** sleep	Ama **goes to** sleep	

Table 2.11: Near future tense.

2.2.5 Indicate the opposite of the action

In general, adding **nn** [**negative marker**] directly in front of the verb tense indicates the action did not take place [**negation**]. When the verb starts with *b*, *p*, *f*, or *m* then an **mm** is used instead.

	Affirmative	Negative
Present	da	nnda
Continous	reda	rennda
Past	daee	annda
Perfect	ada	nndaee
Future	bɛda	mmbɛda
Near Future	kɔda	nnkɔda

Table 2.12: Forming negations.

Take note of the way the Past and Perfect tenses switch their negative forms!

A good verb conjugation book will give you plenty

of practice in forming negations of the various verb tenses.

2.2.6 Extending Nouns and Verbs

Nouns and verbs can be extended in meaning with additional words.

Noun are extended with **adjectives**. Adjectives are placed after the noun. For example, **dan foforo** [*new house*].

Verb actions can be extended in meaning with **adverbs**. Adverbs are also placed after the verb. For example, **nantew ntɛm** [*walk quickly*]

Adjectives and adverbs have the unique property that they can be repeated for emphasis.

	Adjective	Adverb
Akan	dɛw	ntɛm
English	sweet	quick(ly)
Akan	dɛwdɛw	ntɛmntɛm
English	very sweet	very quick(ly)
Akan	dɛwdɛwdɛw	ntɛmntɛmntɛm
English	very very sweet	very very quick(ly)

Table 2.13: Repeat for emphasis.

2.3   Recognising sentences

2.3.1   Sentence patterns

There are three main sentence patterns in Akan:

- making a statement [**declarative sentences**]
- asking a question [**interrogative sentences**]
- commanding [**imperative sentences**]

Making a statement

e.g. *I love you.*

Akan Word Order	Me	dɔ	wo
Grammar	[Noun]	[Verb]	[Noun]
	required	*required*	*optional*
Literal English	I	love	you

Asking a question

e.g. *How are you?*

Akan Word Order	Ɛ-	te	sɛn?
Grammar	[Noun]	[Verb]	[Interrogative pronoun]
	required	*required*	*required*
Literal English*	It	feels	how?

Commanding

e.g. *Stop making noise!*

Akan Word Order	Gyae	dede-yɛ!
Grammar	[Verb]	[Noun]
	required	*optional*
Literal English*	Stop	noise-making!

2.3.2 Forming complex sentences

Conjunctions allow you to link two or more similar components (e.g. two nouns, or, three verbs, or five sentences). Some common conjunctions are listed in Table 2.14.

Akan	Kofi **nye** Ama	Di **na** da
Literal English	Kofi **with** Ama	Eat **then** sleep
English	Kofi **and** Ama	Eat **and then** sleep
Akan	Kofi **anaa** Ama	Me reda **nti** da
English	Kofi **or** Ama	I am sleeping **so** sleep
Akan	**Sɛ** Yaa ...	**Sɛ** Yaa ba **a**, ...
English	**If** Yaa ...	**If** Yaa comes **then** ...
Akan	**Aber a** me ...	**Sɛ** me da **mpo a** ...
English	**While** I ...	**Even if** I sleep ...

Table 2.14: Common conjunctions.

Prepositions on the other hand are placed after nouns to indicate the position of some other noun. Table 2.15 lists some common prepositions.

Akan	Ɛte sɛ fufu	Ɔte dɛ Kwame
English	It is **like** fufu	He is **like** Kwame
Akan	Kɔ **mu**	Kɔ **ase**
English	Go **in**	Go **down**
Akan	Kɔ **ana** ɔaba	Kɔ **fi** ha
English	Go **before** she comes	Go **from** here
Akan	Twe **bɛn** me	Kɔ **akyi**
English	Come **near** me	Go **behind**

Table 2.15: Common prepositions.

The following sentence patterns therefore become easy to understand:

Kofi rekɔ sukuu.
Kofi is going to school.

Kofi nye Ama rekɔ sukuu.
Kofi and Ama are going to school.

Kofi nye Ama reda ansa wɔn akɔ sukuu.
Kofi and Ama are sleeping before they go to school.

Chapter 3

Writing Akan

The Akan Orthography Committee, in 1968, recommended a uniform written form [**orthography**] for Asante Twi, Akuapem Twi and Fanti. In 2003, the uniform orthography was extended to cover the Akan languages of Ivory Coast as well [4]. This implements the uniform orthography under the general name Modern Akan, or simply, Akan.

The philosophy behind this updated orthography is that written Akan should be more predictable than spoken Akan, yet be sufficiently pliable to allow the writer to capture shades of meaning without undue exertion. Thus Modern Akan strives to achieve a noticeable aesthetic of simplicity of form and elegance of construction as exemplified by the great proverbs of the Akan people.

3.1 Spelling conventions

The following spelling conventions are supported by the spellchecker available from the Akan language resources page at `http://kasahorow.org/akan`.

3.2 General guidelines

- Do not use accents on top of vowels [**diacritics**]. Instead structure your sentences to avoid ambiguity. For example, write **Adaka A so sen adaka B** [*Box A is bigger than box B*] instead of **Adaka A sõ sen adaka B***. The version without diacritics is easier to write and just as clear and unambiguous.

- There should never be more than two vowels written side by side in a word. Therefore, where a grammar rule generates three consecutive vowels, the last vowel is not written. For example, write **bae** instead of **baee*** when conjugating the verb **ba**.

- Do not use elliptical forms. Write **Me aba fie** [*I have come home*] instead of **M'aba fie*** or **Maba fie***. This serves the purpose of making text easier to break down after a single read (Table 3.1).

Akan	Me	a	ba	fie
Grammar	Pronoun	Perfect tense indicator	Verb	Noun
English	I	have	come	home

Table 3.1: Breaking down a sentence from the written form.

- Include the appropriate silent vowel that is typically pronounced if the word is enunciated slowly. For example, **soro** [*sky*] instead of **sor***, **kurow** [*town*] instead of **kro***

- Use *mb-* instead of *mm-**, *nd-* instead of *nn-**. **Mbarima** [*males*], **ndeɛma** [*things*] are preferred to **mmarima*** or **nneɛma***

- Hyphenate duplicate words. For example **nkurow-nkurow** [*towns*] is preferred to **nkurownkurow***

- Hyphenate words joined together to form a single concept to clarify the composition of the new concept. For example, **mbrahyɛ-begua** [*house of parliament*] is preferred to **mbrahyɛbegua***

- For titles, capitalize only the first character. For example, write **Fa ka ho** [*Add to it*] instead of **Fa Ka Ho***.

3.3   Importing foreign words

- Import into Akan, without a change of spelling, specialised terminology unlikely to come into popular usage. This eliminates the possibility of ambiguity for specialists who are already familiar with the term.

  It is good practice to indicate the origin of the specialized terminology. For example,
  Gold (Borɔfo) yɛ sika [*Gold (English) is money*]

- Phonetically render into Akan new words likely to come into popular usage or likely to come into popular usage. When doing so, stick to the pronunciation pattern of the original language. This enables readers who encounter the word for the first-time in writing to pronounce the word in a way that will confirm to their ears that it is indeed not an uncommon term. For example, **haedrogyin** [*hydrogen*].

  When words are deemed to have made the transition from specialised terminology into popular usage, this convention should be applied to revise the spelling of the word accordingly.

3.4   Punctuation

pɔw [*fullstop*]	.	Used to indicate the end of a sentence. Also used to separate the whole number and the fraction components of a decimal number like 1.23

Table 3.2: Punctuation.

Chapter 4

Speaking Akan

4.1 Sounds

The sounds in Akan are divided into **vowels** and **consonants**. There are seven vowels in Akan—a ɛ e i ɔ o u—representing ten main vowel sounds as listed in Table 4.1. Nasalized vowels are not included here as you typically don't need them to make yourself understood.

The following sentence contains all the Akan vowel sounds:

Me bɛba afi sukuu no nna ndɔn-asia abɔ.
M/ei/   b/ɛ/b/a/   /ɛy/f/i/   s/u/k/uu/ no nna
nd/ɔ/n-asia abɔ.

Akan writing	Sound	As in
a	/a/	hat
a	/ɛy/	**a** boy
e	/ei/	fit
e	/ay/	s**ay**
ɛ	/ɛ/	hen
i	/i/	feed
o	/o/	af**oot**
o	/oa/	g**oa**t
ɔ	/ɔ/	hot
u	/u/	cool

Table 4.1: Akan vowels and their pronunciation.

The rest of the Akan alphabet represent the consonants. They are enunciated in the same way as the English pronunciation of those letters.

Akan writing	Sound	As in
ɓ	/h/	**b**an
c	/c/	**c**an
d	/d/	**d**in
f	/f/	**f**an
g	/g/	**g**o
h	/h/	**h**i
j	/j/	**j**ut
k	/k/	**k**in
l	/l/	**l**it
m	/m/	**m**um
n	/n/	**n**un
n	/ng/	ali**gn**
p	/p/	**p**un
r	/r/	**r**un
s	/s/	**s**on
t	/t/	**t**on
v	/v/	**v**an
w	/w/	**w**an
y	/y/	**y**es
z	/z/	**z**oo

Table 4.2: Akan consonants and their pronunciation.

Additional consonants are represented by the combinations [**digraphs**] listed in 4.3. The sound combination is enunciated as a single short sound. Not all the combinations have exact correspondents in English pronunciation.

Akan writing	Sound	As in
dw	/dw/	ca**j**un
dz	/dz/	a**dz**e
gy	/gy/	**j**am
hw	/hw/	**wh**o
hy	/hy/	**sh**ine
ks	/x/	ta**x**i
ky	/ky/	ca**tch**
ny	/ny/	ba**ny**an
tw	/tw/	Saska**tchew**an

Table 4.3: Akan digraphs and their pronunciation.

The following sentence contains all the Akan digraphs:

Kwame nn**dw**en **hw**ee **ky**en **gy**ama ta**ks**i no a woa**hy**ɛ no sɛ ɔ**ny**im sɛ ɔre**tw**eɔn no no.

mbox

4.2 Pronouncing Akan languages

To understand the pronunciation tables coming up, remember that

- . represents a consonant sound
- - represents *ends with*
- [a,b]c represents the alternatives *ab* or *ac*
- // represents silence

4.3 Speaking Akuapem Twi

Akuapem Twi is generally pronounced as written with the Modern Akan spelling system.

Rule	Sound	Akan	Akuapem Twi
a.a	/a/	adaka	/a/d**a**ka
a.e	/a/	ase	/a/s**e**
a.ɛ	/a/	abɛn	/a/b**ɛ**n
a.o	/a/	apon	/a/p**o**n
a.ɔ	/a/	adɔyɛ	/a/d**ɔ**yɛ
a.u	/ɛ/	aduane	/ɛy/d**u**ane
a.i	/ɛ/	asia	/ɛy/s**i**a
mb	/m/+/m/	mboa	/mm/oa
nd	/n/+/n/	ndua	/nn/ua
nye	/n/+/ei/	nye	/nei/
nyi	/n/+/i/	nyimpa	/ni/mpa
-ane	/a/+/ng/	aduane	adu/ang/
-n	/ng/	adɛn	adɛ/ng/

Table 4.4: Speaking Akan with Akuapem Twi pronunciation.

4.4 Speaking Asante Twi

Asante Twi is usually spoken about one and half times
more rapidly than Akuapem Twi and Fanti. As a re-
sult, words roll into each other more often when speaking Asante Twi. Many intermediate sounds are also
skipped to enable the faster speaking pace. Speak it
at a higher pitch relative to Akuapem Twi and Fanti.

Rule	Sound	Akan	Asante Twi
a.a	/a/	adaka	/a/daka
a.e	/a/	ase	/a/se
a.ɛ	/a/	abɛn	/a/bɛn
a.o	/a/	apon	/a/pon
a.ɔ	/a/	adɔyɛ	/a/dɔyɛ
a.u	/ɛ/	aduane	/ɛy/duane
a.i	/ɛ/	asia	/ɛy/sia
gu	/dw/	guane	/dw/ane
mb	/m/+/m/	mboa	/mm/oa
nd	/n/+/n/	ndua	/nn/ua
nye	/n/+/ei/	nye	/nei/
nyi	/n/+/i/	nyimpa	/ni/mpa
wô	//	me da wo ase	me da//ase
re	//	me reda	me//eda
bɛ	//	me bɛda	m//ɛda
-ar	/a/	mpasar	mpas/a/
-e	/ei/+/ɛ/	aware	awar/eiɛ/
-ew	/ei/+/ɛ/	afasew	afas/eiɛ/
-i	/i/	firi	fir/i/
-o	/oo/+/ɔ/	sofo	sɔf/ooɔ/
-u	/u/+/o/	afotu	afot/uo/
-w	//	awɔw	awɔ//

Table 4.5: Speaking Akan with Asante Twi pronunciation.

4.5 Speaking Fanti

Fanti is considered the most sedate form of spoken Akan. Along the West African coast, it may be spoken at an even lower pitch than Akuapem Twi.

Rule	Sound	Akan	Fanti
a.a	/a/	adaka	/a/d**a**ka
a.e	/a/	ase	/a/s**e**
a.ɛ	/a/	abɛn	/a/b**ɛ**n
a.o	/a/	apon	/a/p**o**n
a.ɔ	/a/	adɔyɛ	/a/d**ɔ**yɛ
a.u	/e/	aduane	/e/d**u**ane
a.i	/e/	asia	/e/s**i**a
d[i,e]	/dz/	din, de	/dz/in, /dz/e
me re.o	/ei/	me retow	m/oo/ r/oo/t**ow**
me re.i	/ei/	me redi	m/i/ r/i/d**i**
me re.u	/ei/	me resu	m/u/ r/u/s**u**
t[i,e]	/ts/	ti, te	/ts/i, /ts/e
-[m,n,r][e,i,u]	//	ahome, huri, soro	ahom//, hur//, sor//
.e.	//	ahomeka	ahom//ka

Table 4.6: Speaking Akan with Fanti pronunciation.

4.6 Listening to Akan

You should be able to understand most of the other varieties of Akan if you can understand any of Akuapem Twi, Asante Twi, or Fanti.

Typically, if you cannot follow spoken speech, ask the speaker to slow down their rate of talking. At the slower speed, you should be able to pick up enough words to make sense of what is being said. (You only need to ask them to speak louder if they are speaking too softly.)

Chapter 5

Phrase Reference

Here are some handy phrases that you should memorize to fill in the silence while you frantically think of how to say something complicated.

Hello	Ɛ te sɛn?
How are you?	Wo ho te sɛn?
I am fine	Me ho yie
And you?	Na wo so ɛ?
Goodbye	Baebae
Later	Akyiri yi
Good morning	Me ma wo akye
Good afternoon	Me ma wo aha
Good evening	Me ma wo adwo
Good night	Ade nkye o
Sleep well	Da yie

What is your name?	Wɔ frɛ wo sɛn?
My name is Janet	Me din de Janet
I come from France	Me fi Frans
I am a ...	Me yɛ ...
I am a teacher	Me yɛ tikyanyi
I am hungry	Kɔm de me
I am thirsty	Nsukɔm de me
I like/want ...	Me pɛ ...
I don't like/want ...	Me mmpɛ ...
It is a bit expensive	Ne bo yɛ den kakra
It is not expensive	Ne bo nnyɛ den
Yes	Aane
No	Daabi; Aaha
Please	Me pa wo kyɛw
Sorry	Kosɛ
Thank you	Me da wo ase
What is the time?	Wɔ abɔ ahe?
The time is ...	Wɔ abɔ ...
The time is 2 o'clock	Wɔ abɔ ndɔn abien

Chapter 6

Essential Vocabulary

Section 2.3 introduced the sentence patterns in Akan. This section provides basic vocabulary to help you create correctly constructed sentences according to those patterns. Reading Akan texts with the aid of a dictionary [3] will help you round out your vocabulary.

6.1 Names and things

This section introduces some common nouns.

6.1.1 Telling time

The day is divided into 24 **ndɔn** [*hours*] or 5 periods.

Asuom   Wee hours

Ahanamakye	Dawn
Anapa	Morning
Awiabere	Afternoon
Awimbere	Evening
Anafua	Night

6.1.2 Days of the week

The word **ndaawɔtwe** [*eight days*], usually translated *week*, in English refers to any eight-day period starting and ending on the same weekday inclusive, e.g. Tuesday – Wednesday – Thursday – Friday – Saturday – Monday – Tuesday comprise one week.

Kwasida	*Sunday*
Dwowda	*Monday*
Benada	*Tuesday*
Wukuda	*Wednesday*
Yawda	*Thursday*
Fida	*Friday*
Memeneda	*Saturday*

6.1.3 Common names

Most people are called by their day-names--a name that indicates the day of the week on which they were born.

Asi, Esi, Akosua	Sunday female
Kwasi, Kwesi	Sunday male
Adwoa	Monday female
Kwadwo, Kodwo	Monday male
Abena	Tuesday female
Kwabena, Kɔbena	Tuesday male
Akua, Ekua	Wednesday female
Kwaku, Kweku	Wednesday male
Yaa, Aba, Araba	Thursday female
Yaw, Kwaw, Kɔw	Thursday male
Afua, Efua, Afia, Efia	Friday female
Kofi	Friday male
Ama, Amba	Saturday female
Kwame, Kwamena	Saturday male

And here are some common titles that precede Akan names:

Maame, Maa	mother
Papa, Paa	father
Nana	honourable

6.1.4 Numbers

The Akan number system, **nkanee** [*numbers*], is decimal. Fractions are formed using a **abiasa mu abien** [*two out of three*] ($^2/_3$), **akron mu awɔtwe** [*eight out of nine*] ($^8/_9$) pattern. Numbers after a decimal point, **pɔw** [*point*], are always elaborated with the basic 0 to 9 numbers: **hwee pɔw anum** [*zero point five*] (0.5), **hwee pɔw anum hwee anan** [*zero point five zero four*] (0.504). Negative numbers are prefixed with the negative marker **kaw** [*negative*] (-).

hwee	0
koro	1
abien	2
abiasa	3
anan	4
anum	5
asia	6
asuon	7
awɔtwe	8
akron	9
du	10
du-biako	11
du-abien	12
du-abiasa	13
du-anan	14

du-anum	15
du-asia	16
du-asuon	17
du-awɔtwe	18
du-akron	19
aduonu	20
aduonu-biako	21
aduonu-abien	22
aduasa	30
aduanan	40
aduanum	50
aduasia	60
aduasuon	70
aduawɔtwe	80
aduakron	90
ɔha	100
ɔha-na-koro	101
ɔha-na-abien	102
ahaabien	200
ahaabiasa	300
ahaanan	400
ahaanum	500
ahaasia	600
ahaasuon	700
ahaawɔtwe	900
apem	1,000
mpemabien	2,000
mpemabiasa	3,000

mpemdu	10,000
mpemdubiako	11,000
mpem ɔha	100,000
ɔpepepem	1,000,000
ɔpepepepem	1,000,000,000
afebɔɔ	∞

fa	$1/2$
abiasa-mu-koro	$1/3$
abiasa-mu-abien	$2/3$
anan-mu-koro	$1/4$
anan-mu-abiasa	$3/4$
anum-mu-abiasa	$3/5$
koro **pɔw** anan	1.4
hwee **pɔw** abien abiasa asuon	0.237

6.1.5   Directions

bankum	left
nyifa	right
soro	up
ase	down
finimfin	central, middle
atifi	north
anaafo	south
boka	east
anee	west
apuei	easterly

atɔe   westerly

6.1.6   Food

adiban   food
nsu   water
nam   fish, meat
apɔnkye-nam   goat-meat
nsumu-nam   in-water-meat* [*fish*]
frɔwee   gravy, stew
nkwan   soup
bankye   cassava, manioc
borɛde   plantain
aburow   corn, maize
moo   rice

6.1.7   Transportation

trɔtrɔ   minivan
kaar   car
keteke   train

6.1.8   Colours

angoa   yellow
bruu   blue
abunabun   green

fufuw	white
indigo	indigo
kɔkɔɔ	red
ntokowa ntokowa	brown
ɔrenge	orange
pɛpol	purple
tuntum	black

6.1.9   Months

Sanda-Ɔpɛpɔn	January
Kwakwar-Ɔgyefuo	February
Ebɔw-Ɔbenem	March
Ebɔbira-Oforisuo	April
Esusow-Kɔtɔnimba	May
Obiradze-Ayɛwohomumu	June
Ayɛwoho-Kitawonsa	July
Difuu-Ɔsandaa	August
Fankwa-Ɛbɔ	September
Ɔbɛsɛ-Ahinime	October
Ɔberɛfɛw-Obubuo	November
Mumu-Ɔpɛnimba	December

6.1.10   Family

abusua	family
papa	father

maame	mother
ba	child
nua	sibling
nua-banyin	brother
nua-basia	sister

6.1.11 Occupations

okuanyi	farmer
pofonyi	fisherman
nɛɛsenyi	nurse
dɔketanyi	doctor
tikyanyi	teacher
kyerɛwnyi	journalist
adetɔnnyi	trader
sɔfo	pastor

6.2   Actions

Here is a quick refresher on verbs and their tenses.

Present: present tense
Me <u>da</u> [*I sleep*]

Past: simple past tense
Me <u>daee</u> ndeda [*I slept yesterday*]

Perfect: present perfect tense
Me <u>ada</u> [*I am asleep*]

Future: simple future tense
Me <u>bɛda</u> [*I will sleep*]

Continuous: present continuous tense
Me <u>reda</u> [*I am sleeping*]

Negation: negative form of present tense
Me <u>nnda</u> [*I do not sleep*]

Subjunctive: a verb form used to express wishes, emotion, possibility, judgment, opinion, necessity
Yɛ <u>nda</u> [*Let us sleep*]

Participle: noun describing the action of the verb
<u>Nda</u> yie [*Sleeping is good*]

Gerund: noun describing the possessive action of the verb
Ne <u>ndae</u> mber yɛ tia [Its *sleeping* period is short]

The form of a verb used to command, the **imperative**, is just the verb root by itself. Some verbs have a different form of the imperative. The most common exception is the verb **ba** [*come*] whose imperative form is **bra**. The imperative form does not have a subject. ı.e.

Bra ha! [*Come* here!]

Kofi se, **da**. [Kofi says, *sleep*.]

6.2.1   Simple verbs

Simple verbs are words which stand alone and are conjugated by themselves. They end in any of the seven vowels, or **m, n, r, w**.

ba [*come*]

kɔ [*go*]

di [*eat*]

nom [*drink*]

kan [*count*]

kenkan [*read*]

kyerɛw [*write*]

ma [*give*]

gye [*get*]

fa [*take*]

6.2.2   Compound verbs

Compound verbs are made up of a simple verb root and a verb participle. During conjugation, only the simple verb root is conjugated. See Table 6.1 for the conjugation of a sample compound verb.

Common compound verbs use the following simple verb roots:

da, e.g. **da dinn** [*quieten down*]

fa, e.g. **fa ... adamfo** [*befriend ...*]

gye, e.g. **gye ... di** [*believe ...*]

hyɛ, e.g. **hyɛ nkɔm** [*prophesy*]

ma, e.g. **ma do** [*lift*]

tɔ, e.g. **tɔ nko** [*doze*]

tu, e.g. **tu mpon** [*make progress*]

yi, e.g. **yi ... ano** [*answer ...*]

yɛ, e.g. **yɛ ... atuu** [*embrace ...*]

Table 6.1: **hyɛ** compound verbs.

Present	**hyɛ nkɔm** [*prophesy*]
Past	hyɛee nkɔm

Table 6.1: **hyɛ** compound verbs.

Perfect	ahyɛ nkɔm
Future	bɛhyɛ nkɔm
Continuous	rehyɛ nkɔm
Negation	nnhyɛ nkɔm
Gerund	nkɔmhyɛ

Table 6.2: **tu** compound verbs.

Present	**tu mpon** [*make progress*]
Past	tuee mpon
Perfect	atu mpon
Future	bɛtu mpon
Continuous	retu mpon
Negation	nntu mpon
Gerund	mpontu

6.3 Write and speak whole sentences!

With your new found knowledge, and a dictionary, you should be able to translate the following sentences from Akan and speak them with a Fanti, Akuapem or Asante Twi accent.

1. Me dɔ wo.
2. Ɔyɛ banyin.
3. John baa ha ansa mereba.
4. Woana nye no?
5. Adwoa bɛba fie ɔkyena.
6. Me bae, me hue, me die nkonyim.
7. Wɔ mpɛ dɛm.
8. Mo de ndɔn abien die piza anum?!
9. Abusua no akɔhɛn wɔn fie foforo no mu.
10. Gyae didi na yɛ no ntɛm!

Bibliography

[1] Google et al. *Google search engine in Akan*, 2009. `http://www.google.com/intl/ak/`.

[2] Jojoo Imbeah et al. *Firefox web browser in Akan*, 2009. `http://kasahorow.org/akan/firefox`.

[3] kasahorow Editors. *Modern Akan Dictionary: Akan-English, English-Akan.* kasahorow, 2005.

[4] N'Guessan Jérémie Kouadio, Kofi Korankye Saah Kofi Agyekum, James Gyekye-Aboagye, Kalilou Tera, and Djaban Tano Kouame. *A Unified Orthography for the Akan Languages of Ghana and Ivory Coast – General Spelling Rules.* The Centre for Advanced Studies of African Society (CASAS), 2003.

Index

http://kasahorow.org/books

Pre-School

Me 1 2 3 Nwoma: Kala na Sua
Me A B D Nwoma: Kala na Sua

Basic User

Modern Akan
102 Akan Verbs
Modern Akan Dictionary

Independent User

Mbofragoro
Fa Bi Gye Serew
Baahemaa

Proficient User

Afriyie

Lightning Source UK Ltd.
Milton Keynes UK
UKHW022152070921
390162UK00011B/2450

9 789988 037673